D0323998

COUNTDOWN TO SPACE

COUNTDOWN TO SPACE

EARTH—
THE THIRD PLANET

Michael D. Cole

Series Advisors:
Marianne J. Dyson
Former NASA Flight Controller
and
Gregory L. Vogt, Ed. D.
NASA Aerospace Educational Specialist

Enslow Publishers, Inc.

40 Industrial Road	PO Box 38
Box 398	Aldershot
Berkeley Heights, NJ 07922	Hants GU12 6BP
USA	UK

http://www.enslow.com

Library of Congress Cataloging-in-Publication Data

Cole, Michael D.
    Earth—the third planet / Michael D. Cole.
       p. cm. — (Countdown to space)
    Includes bibliographical references and index.
    Summary: Describes the third planet from the sun, including its orbit,
seasons, gravity, geology, and life.
    ISBN 0-7660-1507-6
    1. Earth—Juvenile literature. [1. Earth.] I. Title. II. Series.
QB631.4 .C65 2001
525—dc21

                                                    00-009188

Printed in the United States of America

10 9 8 7 6 5 4 3 2

Illustration Credits: Courtesy Calvin J. Hamilton, p. 15; © Corel
Corporation, pp., 32, 33, 36; Enslow Publishers, Inc., p. 21; National
Aeronautics and Space Administration (NASA), pp. 4, 9, 11, 12, 16, 18–19,
23, 25, 27, 30, 38, 39, 41; Russian Information Office, p. 6; Illustration by
Michael W. Skrepnick ©1998, p. 35.

Cover Illustration: NASA (foreground); Raghvendra Sahai and John
Trauger (JPL), the WFPC2 science team, NASA, and AURA/STScI
(background).

CONTENTS

Cosmonaut Yuri Gagarin was the first human being to set his eyes on the surface of the planet Earth from space. This photo shows part of the East Coast of the United States.

1

"I See the Earth"

The countdown at the Tyuratum launch site in the Soviet Union had reached zero. Yellow flames suddenly gushed from the engines of the mighty Vostok rocket. The launchpad shook and the engines roared as the rocket thundered into the sky.

It was April 12, 1961. Soviet cosmonaut Yuri Gagarin was on his way into space.

No human had gone into space before. Gagarin was about to become the first. His Vostok rocket carried him higher and higher through the atmosphere. The air was becoming thinner and thinner. Minutes after the launch, Gagarin's spacecraft separated from the rocket. The metal covering that protected the spacecraft during launch was then let loose.

"The fairing has been discarded," Gagarin said.[1]

Gagarin could now look out his spacecraft's window. There was no more sky above him. There was only the darkness of space. But below him was a sight no human had seen before.

"I see the Earth," Gagarin said.[2]

Cosmonaut Yuri Gagarin smiles with delight as the first human to orbit our planet.

Yuri Gagarin was the first human to see his home planet from space. His spacecraft was in orbit, traveling around Earth at 17,500 miles per hour. As Gagarin watched from his spacecraft, whole continents and oceans passed below him. He could see the entire course of rivers and follow great mountain ranges. Gagarin passed rapidly over his home country of Russia. In just ninety minutes, he was able to orbit, or go around, the entire Earth.

"The sky looks very, very dark," he said, "and the Earth is bluish."[3]

To the space travelers who have followed Gagarin, especially those who went to the Moon and back, Earth's bluish globe appeared like a life-filled oasis in the darkness of space. The other planets in our solar system are strikingly different from Earth. Some planets are covered with thick atmospheres of poisonous gas. Other planets have little atmosphere at all.

Scientists have been sending robotic spacecraft to the other planets since the early 1960s. Scientists continue to search for evidence of life, past or present, on the other planets and moons in our solar system.

So far, only Earth, the third planet from the Sun, thrives with life. The existence of so many forms of life makes Earth a very dynamic planet.

2

Discovering a Remarkable Planet

Yuri Gagarin was right. Earth is definitely bluish.

The blue oceans that cover most of our planet make it unique in our solar system. Water is an essential component for the existence of life. Oceans cover 70 percent of Earth, and the planet's clouds are made of water vapor, which rains back down to the surface.

But people did not always think of Earth and its oceans the way that they do today. As recently as a few hundred years ago, most people believed that Earth was flat. They thought that ships and their crews sailing too far out into the ocean would fall off the edge of the planet.

The effort to learn about Earth's nature and origin began with the work of ancient astronomers nearly four thousand years ago. Their observations of objects in the sky would eventually lead to an understanding of what Earth is and how it relates to the rest of the universe.

Early astronomers in China, Babylon, Egypt, and Greece observed that the Sun, the Moon, and the stars moved through the sky quite differently. These astronomers also identified a set of five other objects. The five rather bright objects looked like stars, but over the course of weeks and months, they were observed to move through the sky independently against the background of stars. Curiously, the objects sometimes appeared to stop and move backward in relation to the

The blue Earth is covered with life-sustaining water.

stars around them, before resuming their gradual movement across the sky from west to east.

These objects were given the name *planetes*, which is Greek for "wanderers." It is the basis for the English word *planet*. Early astronomers recorded the movements of the planets Mercury, Venus, Mars, Jupiter, and Saturn. Because they were dim, the planets Uranus, Neptune, and Pluto were not discovered until long after the development of telescopes.

The Greeks also became quite certain that Earth was round, not flat. Their calculations of Earth's size were very close to the actual size of Earth, which is about 8,000 miles in diameter.[1]

The Greek astronomer Ptolemy wrote that the round Earth is the center of the universe, and that the planets, stars, Sun, and Moon are orbiting around it. For many centuries, people believed that Earth was the center of the universe. But in 1473, Nicolaus Copernicus published his book claiming that the planets orbit around the Sun. Earth, he said, is another planet, like Mercury, Venus, Mars, Jupiter, and Saturn. Johannes Kepler later proved that the Sun-centered model of the solar system is correct. After thousands of years of searching to understand the solar system, the most important discovery of these early astronomers was the discovery about Earth.[2]

In modern times, scientists have studied Earth and our solar system by sending spacecraft into Earth-orbit

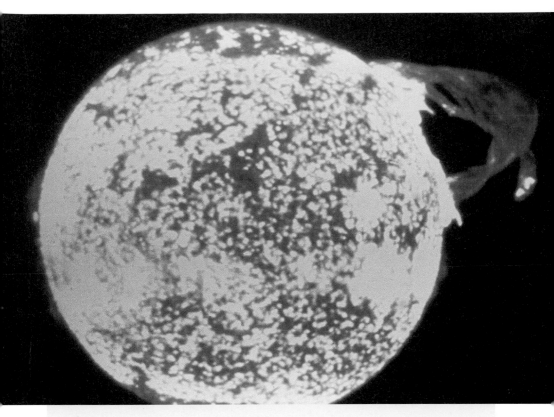

Johannes Kepler proved that the Sun, shown here with an erupting surface, is the center of the solar system.

and to visit the other planets. The knowledge gained by the voyages of these spacecraft proved that within our solar system, Earth is a remarkably unique world.

Surface Conditions

Earth is the only known planet with an average surface temperature that is between the freezing and boiling points of water.[3] Water's freezing point is 32° F (0° C), while its boiling point is 212° F (100° C). There are of

11

course polar ice caps where the water always remains frozen, and there are seasons on Earth when the temperature can dip well below freezing. But the temperature on Earth's surface never reaches the 212° F boiling point.

Earth's Orbit

Earth's circular orbit around the Sun helps to maintain its surface temperature. It orbits at a distance of 93 million miles from the Sun. If Earth orbited much farther from the Sun, its average temperature would be much colder. If it orbited nearer the Sun, its average temperature would likely be much warmer.

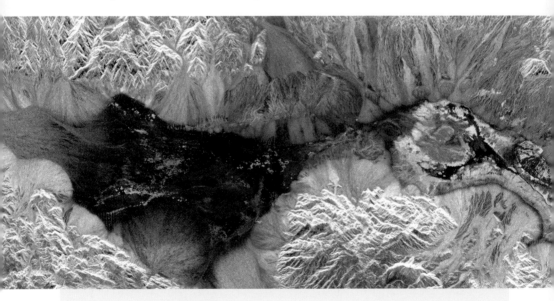

Earth is one of the four terrestrial planets in our solar system. These planets are made of rock. This stunning radar image taken from the space shuttle shows the mountains of Death Valley, California. The bright mountains surround dark basins and valleys.

Earth is one of the terrestrial planets, which means it is a planet made of rock. Mercury, Venus, and Mars are the other terrestrial planets. Jupiter, Saturn, Uranus, and Neptune are giant planets made up mostly of gases. The planet Pluto is a tiny world made of rock and ice. With a diameter of nearly 8,000 miles (13,000 kilometers) at its equator, Earth is the largest terrestrial planet. Venus is slightly smaller, at about 7,500 miles (12,000 kilometers) in diameter. Mars is a little more than half Earth's size, at 4,200 miles (6,700 kilometers) in diameter. Mercury is smallest, with a diameter of just over 3,000 miles (4,800 kilometers).

Earth's Layers

The rocky structure of Earth consists of four main layers. Although scientists have never directly observed these layers, their study of earthquakes and the way earthquake waves move through Earth have led them to their current picture of what the interior of the planet must be like.

At the center of Earth is a hot, solid inner core. This core is probably made of iron and nickel. Its estimated temperature is about 9,000° F (5,000° C). This core is solid because of the tremendous pressure placed upon it by the hundreds of miles of material pressing down on it from above. About 760 miles from the center of Earth, the surrounding outer core is liquid. The outer core also consists mostly of iron and nickel, and is about 1,800 miles (3,000 kilometers) thick.[4]

The partly liquid mantle layer surrounds the core. It accounts for 67 percent of Earth's mass. It is more than 1,400 miles thick and is made up of hot, dense, but somewhat movable rock material. Its temperature ranges between 5,400° F (3,000° C) in the lower mantle, to 2,700° F (1,500° C) in the mantle just below the crust, which is Earth's outer surface.[5]

On average, the crust is about twenty miles thick but varies in depth from one place to another. Below mountain ranges the crust can be as much as forty miles thick. Beneath the ocean, the crust can be as thin as five miles.

The crust includes a lithosphere layer, which is a series of interlocking plates that make up Earth's continents. These plates are called tectonic plates. Molten material welling up from a ridge between two tectonic plates below the Atlantic Ocean causes the plates on either side of the ridge to move to the east and west. The movement of tectonic plates causes earthquakes.

Earthquakes occur all over the world, even beneath the sea. The effects of earthquakes are felt most strongly near the boundaries of two tectonic plates. When cities are located near such boundaries, and an earthquake occurs, the results can be disastrous.

In 1999, a major earthquake shook the city of

Istanbul in Turkey. Parts of the city were left in ruins. Nearly 20,000 people were killed in the quake, and more than 50,000 were injured. The destruction left more than 200,000 people in the city homeless.[6]

Volcanoes Erupt

Volcanoes are another result of the movements and pressures within Earth's interior. Molten rock, or

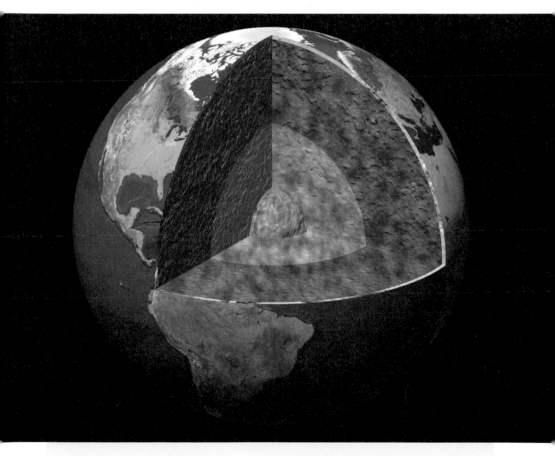

The center of Earth—the inner and outer core—is surrounded by the mantle and then the crust.

magma, welling up within the mantle can burst through the crust and out onto Earth's surface as lava. The piling up of lava can create large mountains on the surface. Volcanic eruptions that occur in the ocean can create a volcanic island or islands. The Hawaiian islands were formed from volcanic eruptions that welled up from the bottom of the Pacific Ocean.

Scientists trying to study volcanoes sometimes have a dangerous job. In 1991, a team of scientists was studying the gigantic eruption of Mount Pinatubo in the Philippine Islands. From fifteen miles away, they watched as the eruption threw thousands of tons of ash and dust ten miles into the sky. After three days the molten rock came crashing down the mountain in

A 1994 radar image from the space shuttle Endeavour *shows Mount Pinatubo in the Philippine Islands. The red color indicates the ash deposited from the 1991 eruptions. The dark areas are the mudflows, which continued to flood the river valleys after heavy rain.*

chunks. Storms then moved through the area. The ash that had been thrown into the air by the volcano combined with the rain, producing a downpour of mud.

At first, the scientists fled the area. Then, they realized that this was the chance of a lifetime. They turned back, intent on witnessing the major eruption up close. But by the time they got to their base near the volcano, the sky was completely black. Chunks of lava the size of golf balls pelted them. They realized they could die! They wisely decided to retreat to a safer distance to monitor the frothing volcano. Fortunately, their previous warnings about the eruption probably saved thousands of lives.[7]

The surface of Earth is clearly affected by the forces and pressures within it. It is equally shaped by its surrounding atmosphere and the particular path the planet takes through space.

EARTH

Age
About 4.5 billion years

Diameter
7,930 miles (12,760 kilometers)

Distance from Sun
93,000,000 miles (150,000,000 kilometers)

Distance to Moon
About 240,000 miles (386,000 kilometers)

Orbital period
365 days and 6 hours

Rotation period
23 hours and 56 minutes

Temperature range
About 120° F (50° C) in parts of Australia and Africa
to about -128° F (-90° C) in parts of Antarctica

Terrestrial composition
Iron and nickel core; semiliquid iron and nickel mantle;
crust of various rock materials

Atmospheric composition
78 percent nitrogen; 20 percent oxygen;
one percent argon; one percent water vapor

Thickness of atmosphere
About 60 miles (100 kilometers), traces beyond

Tilt of planet's axis
23.5 degrees

Estimated lifespan
About 10–11 billion years

First appearance of microscopic cell life
3.5 billion years ago

First appearance of complex multicelled organisms
600 million years ago

First appearance of man
2 million years ago

Number of continents
7 (North America, South America, Europe, Asia,
Australia, Africa, Antarctica)

Number of oceans
4 (Pacific Ocean, Atlantic Ocean, Indian Ocean, Arctic Ocean)

Deepest ocean
Pacific, 36,000 feet (11,000 meters) deep along Mariana Trench

Highest mountain
Mount Everest in Nepal, 29,000 feet (9,000 meters)

Largest city
Mexico City, 8.2 million people

3

The Air Above and the Space Beyond

As Earth travels through space in its orbit around the Sun, it also rotates. Earth's rotation on its axis is like a basketball spinning on someone's fingertip. A day on Earth lasts twenty-four hours because it takes the planet twenty-four hours to rotate once on its axis. This rotation causes the change from day to night. The side of Earth that faces the Sun experiences day, while the side facing away from the Sun experiences night.

Viewed from Earth's North Pole, the planet rotates counterclockwise. This motion causes the Sun to rise in the east and set in the west. Also viewed from the North Pole, Earth orbits the Sun in a counterclockwise motion. It takes 365 and one quarter days for Earth to complete one orbit.

Earth's Seasons

During the year, there are four climate changes on Earth. The seasons are not caused by Earth moving closer to or farther from the Sun in its orbit. Although Earth is closer to the Sun during some parts of its orbit, and further away at others, the change of distance is not enough to cause significant changes in Earth's climate.

Seasons are caused by Earth's tilt on its axis. Earth

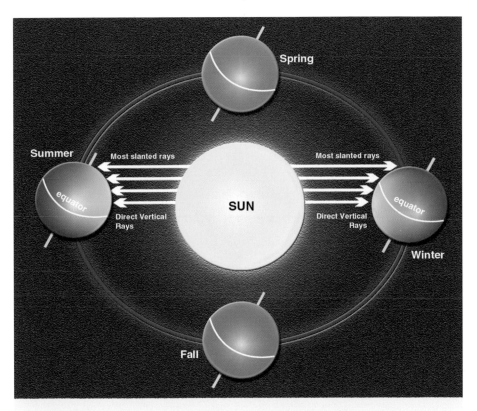

Earth's seasons are caused by the tilt of the planet. When the Northern Hemisphere is tilting toward the Sun, it is summer. In the winter, the Northern Hemisphere is tilting away from the Sun.

does not rotate straight up in relation to the Sun. Instead it rotates at a slight angle. The tilt causes some parts of Earth to receive more direct sunlight for a longer time, creating warmer and longer days. While this is occurring, another part of Earth is receiving less direct sunlight for a shorter period, creating colder and shorter days. Regions near the equator are affected little by the tilt of Earth's axis.

For example, summer occurs in the Northern Hemisphere when it is tilted more directly toward the Sun. Winter occurs in the Northern Hemisphere when it is tilted away from the Sun. The Southern Hemisphere experiences the same seasons but at opposite times of the year.[1]

The Moon

Our Moon orbits Earth from a distance of about 240,000 miles. Most scientists believe the Moon was once part of Earth but was blasted away billions of years ago by the impact of a giant asteroid or comet. However, no one knows for certain.

What is certain is that the Moon's gravity exerts a pull on the oceans, creating the ocean tides. The tides cause minor, temporary shifts in water levels along ocean shorelines. As the Moon orbits Earth, the Moon's gravity raises an oceanic bulge on the side of Earth facing the Moon. The force of Earth's rotation then raises another oceanic bulge on the side opposite the Moon. These

From 240,000 miles away, the Earth is seen rising over the Moon.

bulges on either side of Earth are areas of high tide, while the areas between them are areas of low tide.[2]

Earth's Atmosphere and Weather

Earth's atmosphere surrounds the entire planet. The atmosphere is made mostly of nitrogen, oxygen, and water vapor. Scientists have divided the atmosphere into four different layers. The troposphere is the first layer, closest to the ground. Its average height is about eight miles. Next comes the stratosphere, which extends to about thirty miles above Earth's surface. Most of the ozone is located in this layer. Ozone absorbs much of the harmful ultraviolet light from the Sun and prevents it from reaching the surface. The mesosphere extends to a height of about fifty miles. The thermosphere is the last layer, reaching as high as seventy miles above Earth's surface.

Earth's changing temperatures during the seasons cause weather patterns across the planet. These changes in temperature and pressure cause water to evaporate into the air from oceans and lakes. The water vapor collects in the form of clouds. Most clouds drift about six miles above Earth's surface, although some form at only a few thousand feet. Fog is a cloud that forms on the ground. Sometimes clouds develop into rainclouds or large storm systems. This cycle of evaporation, cloud formation, and rainfall is essential to the existence of life on Earth.

The movement of warm and cold air across the planet's surface is also important. The global system of winds that accomplishes this air movement is called the jet stream. The jet stream moves in a wavy pattern around the Earth, moving warm air from the equator toward the poles, and moving cold air from the poles toward the equator. These rivers of air help maintain the planet's average temperature.

Jet streams are closely monitored by weather forecasters to help determine how weather systems will develop and move. Airline flights across the Atlantic Ocean are planned so that they can take advantage of the jet stream's strong tail winds when flying eastward, such

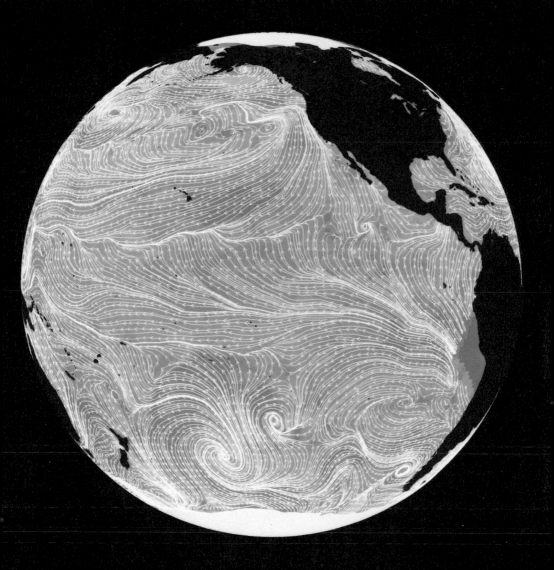

WIND SPEED, M/S

JPL

| 0 | 2 | 4 | 6 | 8 | 10 | 12 | 14 | 16 | 18 | 20 |

Ucla

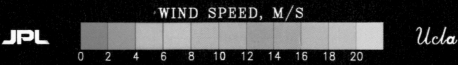

Data from NASA's satellite Seasat shows wind speed in colors and wind direction with arrows. The slowest wind speed is in blue (2–9 miles per hour) and the fastest speed is shown in yellow (35–43 miles per hour). Notice the high-speed winds near Alaska and in the South Pacific.

as from North America to Europe. Airlines also try to avoid the jet stream's strong headwinds when flying westward.[3]

The jet stream, pressure changes, cloud formation, and rainfall sometimes combine to form weather systems that can be very destructive.

When conditions are right in the tropical regions of Earth, storms can develop over the ocean into powerful circular systems of wind and rain called hurricanes, or typhoons. These large weather systems can be hundreds of miles in diameter and can be seen easily from space by satellites or orbiting astronauts. From space, a hurricane looks like a large, swirling mass of clouds. When hurricanes reach land, the strong winds moving around the weather system can cause widespread destruction to property and sometimes death to people living along the coastline. As it moves inland, the hurricane loses force and breaks up. The remainder of the storm is more like a regular rainstorm.[4]

As hurricanes and other weather systems show, Earth's atmosphere and its oceans produce our planet's climate. The oceans are cooled when they release moisture to the atmosphere, and the atmosphere is heated by this added moisture. Oceans also absorb heat from the Sun and prevent the planet from becoming too hot.

The interaction between the atmosphere and ocean currents near the equator produces a system of winds called trade winds. Upwelling cold water in the Pacific

As seen from space, a hurricane is a swirling mass of clouds.

Ocean normally causes surface currents to flow westward from the west coast of South America toward the east coast of Australia. The trade winds also blow to the west.

Every two to seven years, enough warm surface water collects in the middle of the Pacific Ocean to cause a change. It is called an El Niño. Storms are created in the area of the warm surface water, and the surface current and trade winds reverse direction. The El Niño causes global weather changes, such as droughts in Australia and Indonesia. Floods and mudslides occur on the west coast of South America. The El Niño of 1998 caused many problems in the fishing industry. Many kinds of fish die when the change in ocean current suppresses the upwelling of nutrient-rich water from below. Farmers in the central United States also suffered drought conditions in 1998 as a result of El Niño.[5]

The wide-reaching effects of a seemingly small change, such as the reversal of trade winds in an El Niño, show the delicate balance of conditions in our planet's environment. It is in this environment, unlike any other in our solar system, that life has emerged and thrived.

Earth, with its warm temperatures, abundant water, and protective atmosphere, did not become a cradle for life overnight. It took billions of years. To understand how Earth became what it is today, we must start at its beginning.

4

The Ancient Story
of Earth

About 4.5 billion years ago, our solar system began to
form. It began as a vast cloud of gas and dust in space.
Over millions of years, parts of the gas and dust slowly
came together at the center of the cloud. Gravity and
other forces continued to draw parts of the cloud toward
the center, until it became a hot, massive ball of gas.
Eventually the pressure and heat inside the ball of gas
became so great that nuclear reactions were set off inside
it. The ball of gas began to shine as our Sun.

Far out from the center, some of the other gases and
dust in the original dust cloud had clumped together.
These clumps, which eventually became the planets, had
come together far enough from the young Sun to not be
melted by its heat. As one of these bodies grew larger, its

gravity attracted more and more dust and other nearby clumps of material that were forming in space. It grew to the size of a mountain, getting still larger, until gravitational forces molded it into the shape of a sphere. The mass of this rocky world increased until it grew hot on the inside, causing the materials of the new planet to melt and separate. Iron and nickel melted and sank to the core. The rest of the materials moved outward from the core to make up the planet's mantle, or rose all the way to the surface to make up the crust.[1]

The young planet Earth cooled for millions of years. As it cooled, the atmosphere formed from gases released from the hot interior. The gases came through bubbling volcanoes all over the planet. The volcanoes released hydrogen, nitrogen, carbon dioxide, and water vapor, which gradually formed the early atmosphere around the

This painting is an artist's interpretation of the beginning of the universe. Energy and hot matter were sent in all directions. Stars and galaxies formed. Billions of years later, our Sun was formed, along with the nine planets.

planet. As the amount of water vapor in the atmosphere increased, the water began to fall to Earth in the form of rain. After millions of years, enough rain had fallen from the atmosphere to form Earth's oceans. The oceans helped keep Earth's temperature stable. The conditions were in place for early life to thrive.[2]

Life on Earth

Scientists have found fossils of simple microscopic cell life dating back 3.5 billion years. But complex organisms do not appear in the fossil record until just 600 million years ago. That may mean that Earth was already 3.9 billion years old before complex organisms began to thrive. In the millions of years that followed, all life, including plants and animals, began to spread throughout Earth's land and oceans.

Life was thriving on Earth, but things were not always perfect. Over the millions of years, life met some serious challenges. The conditions that allow life to exist on Earth are in a very delicate balance. It takes very little change in these conditions to cause parts of the planet to become too cold or too hot. In the 600 million years since life began to thrive on Earth, this balance of conditions has been upset a number of times.

Slight changes in Earth's orbit or the tilt of its axis have caused colder time periods. Huge sheets of ice, called glaciers, formed over much of the planet. During ice ages, areas nearer the equator remained free of the

Glaciers formed on Earth during the ice ages. Today, the North and South Poles are what remain of the ice age.

glaciers. But the long periods of colder temperatures caused ice to form over a much larger area of the planet than we see today. At Earth's North Pole is the icy Arctic region, and the continent of Antarctica covers the South Pole. These two polar ice caps are what remain of Earth's ice ages after the glaciers receded.[3]

The Great Lakes in North America are also a product of the most recent ice age, which occurred about ten thousand years ago. The five Great Lakes in the northeastern United States are the result of glaciers that melted after carving up their surrounding landscape.

Earth's continents were all connected at one time. But over millions of years, the continents drifted apart, slowly moving over the surface of the planet. As the continents drifted, parts of the land became very warm and dry. These areas, called deserts, are unsuitable for many forms of life. The lack of rain that creates a desert is due to many factors. Atmospheric high pressure areas and cold water currents welling up from the ocean depths in coastal areas have contributed to the formation of deserts.[4]

Glaciers and deserts were produced by gradual changes that occur over hundreds of thousands or millions of years. Challenges to life on Earth have not always been so gradual.

Extinction on Earth

The impacts on Earth from asteroids and comets from outer space have been dramatic and destructive. Geological evidence suggests that at least four times since life began on Earth, the planet has been struck by asteroids large enough to cause the extinction of many forms of life. These mass extinctions were caused by the vast amount of debris that was

Dry, warm desert areas on Earth do not get much rain and are not suitable to many life forms.

thrown up into Earth s atmosphere following the impact of an asteroid that was miles wide. Scientists explain that the resulting dust cloud from such an impact would have covered much of the planet, darkening the sky and lowering Earth s temperature for as long as several years.

One mass extinction occurred about 65 million years ago. Many scientists believe that an asteroid six miles wide struck the Earth and blew so much debris into the air that most of the Sun s light was blocked for a period of months or years. The element iridium is found in Earth s layer from the mass extinction period 66 million years ago. Iridium is ten thousand times more abundant in meteorites and asteroids than in Earth s crust. The iridium may be part of the asteroid that exploded on impact and later settled over parts of Earth with the other dust and debris from the impact.[5]

It is estimated from fossil records that 75 percent of all plant and animal species on Earth were wiped out by the effects of the impact. The dinosaurs were the most notable victims. Only the fossilized remains of these great reptiles exist today. The fossilized skeletons tell us much about dinosaurs and how they lived in the age before the giant asteroid hit Earth.[6]

Despite ice ages and asteroids, life rebounded on Earth again and again. The planet features a variety of environments in which life exists. Scientists estimate that there are more than 20 million species of plants and

An asteroid's collision with Earth may have caused the extinction of the dinosaurs 65 million years ago. However, we are still surrounded by birds, which scientists believe are modern relatives of dinosaurs.

animals on Earth today. Deserts are home to the fewest types of life, while rainforests and wetland areas contain the most. Tropical rainforests may contain 40 percent of all the different animals and plants on the planet. There are 4,000 species of trees alone in the rainforest of South America.[7]

The oceans are also teeming with life, from giant blue whales to microscopic plankton. A vast variety of underwater plants also exist in the oceans. These creatures and plants exist in a saltwater environment, but the world's lakes and streams are filled with fresh water. An entirely different collection of plants, fish, and other creatures survive in fresh water. The Great Lakes are the largest collection of fresh water in the United

States. The largest lake in the world, Lake Baykal in Siberia, contains 20 percent of the world's fresh water.

Eventually a form of life appeared on Earth that walked upright and used its hands to make tools. This species developed languages because its members needed to communicate with each other about how to live and survive. This was the human race—beings with brains capable of asking questions about the mysterious and wondrous world on which they lived.

Life not only exists on the surface of our planet, but in Earth's oceans and freshwater lakes and streams.

5

A World Suitable for Humans

When speaking of Earth, humans can definitely claim there is no place like home.

Nowhere else in the solar system could humans survive for even a few minutes without the aid of a spacesuit. Humans are able to survive comfortably only on Earth.

The presence of oxygen in Earth's atmosphere is one of the most important conditions for human life. Humans need oxygen to breathe. No other planet in the solar system has an atmosphere that contains the amount of oxygen we need. Because plants produce oxygen, a planet will likely have to have abundant plant life before it can provide enough oxygen in the atmosphere for humans and other animals to breathe.

Earth's atmosphere contains the oxygen we need to breathe.

All the Right Conditions

Humans are adapted to Earth's atmospheric pressure. Atmospheric pressure is the weight of the atmosphere above pressing down on us. On Earth's surface, the atmospheric pressure is 14.7 pounds of pressure per square inch. Humans do not experience this pressure as being "heavy." In fact, humans are not actively aware of this pressure at all. But it is certainly there. Humans cannot exist without it.

If Earth's atmospheric pressure were to greatly increase or decrease, strange and dangerous things would happen to the human body. If pressure decreased enough, gases dissolved in our blood would bubble out of the bloodstream and eventually cause death. This would happen quickly if an astronaut's spacesuit ever tore open in space, where there is no pressure at all.

Earth's gravity keeps humans safely on the surface of our planet. Without it, people might leap into the air like Superman and not come down. Gravity on the Moon is only one sixth the gravity on Earth. Astronauts on the Moon had to learn a different way of walking in lighter gravity. They learned a way of hopping to get from place

When astronauts traveled to the Moon, they wore spacesuits. The suits were their "atmosphere" with all the right pressure, temperature, and oxygen conditions humans need to live.

to place. Humans are very adaptable. They have even learned to survive in space where there is no gravity.

Humans are a product of evolution of life on Earth. If the conditions of atmosphere, pressure, gravity, climate, and geology on Earth had been different, humans would have evolved in a different way. In fact, they may not have evolved at all. Millions of years into the future, the environmental conditions on Earth will be different. In order to survive, all living things, including humans, will have to change.

A Changing World

Earth will gradually become warmer as the Sun, in a later stage of its life, enlarges. If humans still exist on Earth at that time, they will have to adapt somehow to the changing environment. Some plants and animals will evolve, while others will die out. Humans will have to live on the surviving species of plants and animals.[1]

Some 4 or 5 billion years from now, heat from the expanding Sun will slowly evaporate the oceans. Earth's atmosphere will escape into space. A dead planet is all that will remain. Eventually the Sun's fiery globe will grow large enough to completely engulf our home world.[2]

Earth will be no more.

That day is far, far into the distant future. It is hoped that our human descendants will have moved on long before then. For now, the Earth is our home, as it is likely to be for millions of years. So far, humanity knows of no other planet like it.

The third planet from the Sun is a place where a delicate balance of conditions, unique in our solar system, has resulted in an amazing variety of life. We, the human species, can count ourselves as one of the most unique features that make up the remarkable planet Earth.

CHAPTER NOTES

Chapter 1. "I See the Earth"

1. Peter Bond, *Heroes in Space: From Gagarin to Challenger* (New York: Basil Blackwell Ltd., 1987), p. 15.

2. Ibid.

3. Martin Caidin, *The Astronauts* (New York: E. P. Dutton and Company, 1961), p. 185.

Chapter 2. Discovering a Remarkable Planet

1. Thomas R. Watters, *Smithsonian Guides: Planets* (New York: Macmillan Publishing Company, 1995), pp. 16, 17.

2. Patrick Moore, *The Picture History of Astronomy* (New York: Grosset and Dunlap, 1961), pp. 34–38, 43–46.

3. Watters, p. 68.

4. Derek Elsom, *Earth: The Making, Shaping and Workings of a Planet* (New York: Macmillan Publishing Company, 1992), p. 32.

5. Michael Allaby, *Earth: Our Planet and its Resources* (New York: Facts on File, Inc., 1993), pp. 17, 22.

6. Borgna Brunner, *Earthquake Factsheet*, n.d. <http://infoplease.lycos.com/spot/earthquake-turkey1.html> (November 27, 1999).

7. Shawna Vogel, *Naked Earth: The New Geophysics* (New York: Penguin Books, 1995), pp. 9–10.

Chapter 3. The Air Above and the Space Beyond

1. Thomas R. Watters, *Smithsonian Guides: Planets* (New York: Macmillan Publishing Company, 1995), pp. 72, 73.

2. Derek Elsom, *Earth: The Making, Shaping and Workings of a Planet* (New York: Macmillan Publishing Company, 1992), pp. 128–129.

3. Ibid., pp. 154–155.
4. Jean Audouze and Guy Israel, ed., *The Cambridge Atlas of Astronomy* (Cambridge, England: Cambridge University Press, 1996), pp. 97–99.
5. Elsom, pp. 124–125.

Chapter 4. The Ancient Story of Earth

1. Thomas R. Watters, *Smithsonian Guides: Planets* (New York: Macmillan Publishing Company, 1995), p. 69.
2. Ibid., pp. 70–71.
3. Derek Elsom, *Earth: The Making, Shaping and Workings of a Planet* (New York: Macmillan Publishing Company, 1992), pp. 98-100.
4. Ibid., pp. 94, 95.
5. Shawna Vogel, *Naked Earth: The New Geophysics* (New York: Penguin Books, 1995), pp. 200–201.
6. Watters, p. 89.
7. Elsom, p. 24.

Chapter 5. A World Suitable for Humans

1. Carl Koppeschaar, *Astronet: Planetary Nebulae*, n.d., <http://www.xs4all.nl/~carlkop/final.html> (August 11, 1999).
2. Ibid.

GLOSSARY

asteroids—Any rocky object in space that measures between a few hundred feet to several hundred miles in diameter. Most asteroids in our solar system orbit the Sun in a region called the asteroid belt, which is between the orbits of Mars and Jupiter.

atmospheric pressure—The force exerted by air, generally measured in reference to sea level.

comets—Bodies of rock and ice in space that circle the Sun in long elliptical orbits. As they draw nearer to the Sun, the ice is melted away, forming a tail. Comets have struck Earth in the past, and the impact of a comet may have caused the extinction of the dinosaurs.

core—The dense, central region of Earth, made up of iron and nickel.

crust—The solid outer layer of Earth, made up of rock materials and a series of interlocking plates that make up the continents.

earthquake—The movement of a part of Earth's crust caused by the slipping or sliding of the crust along the boundary of two tectonic plates.

elliptical orbit—An orbital path that is shaped like the outline of an egg or an oval.

glaciers—Large rivers of ice.

hurricane—A large tropical storm with high-speed circular winds, accompanied by rain, thunder, and lightning.

lava—The molten rock that comes out of a volcano and spreads over Earth's surface, where it quickly cools and becomes solid.

lithosphere—The solid outer layer of Earth that includes the crust and part of the upper mantle. It is divided into tectonic plates that make up the continents of Earth's surface.

magma—The molten material below the Earth's solid rock surface. It is the material thrust out of a volcano during an eruption. Once the magma reaches Earth's surface, it is called lava.

mantle—The mostly solid layer of Earth between the core and the crust. This layer makes up the majority of Earth's mass.

tectonic plates—The interlocking pieces of Earth's crust that make up the continents. Movement along the boundaries of these plates is what causes earthquakes.

tides—The bulging of Earth's oceans toward opposite sides of the globe, caused by the Moon's gravitational pull on the water. The coastal areas in the regions of the bulge experience high tide, while the areas in between the bulge regions experience low tide.

FURTHER READING

Books

Hall, Cally, ed. *Earth Facts*. New York: DK Publishing, 1995.

Jones, Thomas D., and June A. English. *Mission: Earth—Voyage to the Home Planet*. New York: Scholastic Press, 1996.

Rood, Ronald, ed. *The New York Public Library Incredible Earth: A Book of Answers for Kids*. New York: John Wiley and Sons, Inc., 1996.

Royston, Angela, and Jon Adams. *The Earth: Inside and Out*. Oxford, England: Heinemann Library Publishers, 1997.

Van Rose, Susanna. *Eyewitness Science: Earth*. New York: DK Publishing, 1994.

Zike, Dinah. *Earth Science Book: Activities for Kids*. New York: John Wiley and Sons, 1993.

Internet Addresses

Astronomy for Kids: Earth. n.d. <http://www.dustbunny.com/afk/planets/earth/earth.htm> (April 17, 2000).

NASA's Observatorium. © 1995–1999. <http://observe.arc.nasa.gov/nasa/gallery/image_gallery/earth/earth.html> (April 17, 2000).

Sample, Sharron. *For Kids Only: Earth Science Enterprise*. July 15, 1999. <http://kids.earth.nasa.gov/> (April 17, 2000).

INDEX